Introduction

Blanche Burkett White (1895-1978)

If you're a quilter who appreciates exquisite floral appliqué, this is the book for you. "Grandma's Last Quilt" was lovingly stitched by Blanche Burkett White. Her granddaughter, Ladonna Lechner, says that she has only a few pictures of her grandmother because, "Grandma seemed to always be the one taking the pictures."

Born in 1895 near Cedarvale, Kansas, Blanche Burkett became a quilter who was well-known locally for her outstanding workmanship. She lived with her husband, William White, in Grenola, Kansas, where they owned the White Eagle filling station. Ladonna remembers that they had a nice home which her grandmother kept immaculate. Blanche was an excellent cook, had quite a green thumb, and always had a quilt in the quilting frame. Eventually her sons, Kent and Paul, bought an electric quilting machine for their mother, but she never cared for it and continued quilting by hand. Blanche attended the local quilting bee but preferred to do all of the stitching on her own quilts herself. She won many ribbons for her workmanship at the county fair and, as her reputation as a quilter grew, she made quilts for individuals in other states upon request.

When Ladonna Lechner sent a photo of Blanche's final quilt to the Chitra Publications office, we were entranced. Blanche's charming and expertly made quilt is really something special. Knowing quilters would love to see this exceptional quilt and reproduce it for their own enjoyment, we were thrilled when Ladonna decided to share it with you by allowing us to publish "Grandma's Last Quilt."

You'll find the full-size, precise template patterns and clear directions make it easy to stitch all 25 blocks. If you would like to make a fast project, any one of the blocks would make a lovely pillow top or would look impressive quilted and framed. Should you fall in love with one or two specific blocks, simply make several duplicates and turn them into a quilt, or appliqué all 25 blocks and make a replica of the original design. So turn the page and savor each lovely floral block. You're sure to enjoy stitching them into your own family heirloom.

The editors of *Traditional Quiltworks* magazine

The editorial team, clockwise from the top, Jack Braunstein, Debra Feece, Deborah Hearn, Elsie Campbell and Joyce Libal

Table of Contents

For easy reference, we have assigned a letter to each block in the quilt. Block patterns are listed by row, beginning in the upper left corner of the quilt as shown on page 6. Read the *General Directions* on pages 4 and 5 before cutting fabric for the blocks.

General Directions 4
Pattern Pieces 19

Row 1
Block A 7
Block B 7
Block C 8
Block D 8
Block E 9

Row 2
Block F 9
Block G 10
Block H 10
Block I 11
Block J 11

Row 3
Block K 12
Block L 12
Block M 13
Block N 13
Block O 14

Row 4
Block P 14
Block Q 15
Block R 15
Block S 16
Block T 16

Row 5
Block U 17
Block V 17
Block W 18
Block X 18
Block Y 19

General Directions

ABOUT THE PATTERNS
Read through all directions. The pattern pieces do not include seam allowances and are full size, unless otherwise noted. An "R" means the piece will be reversed and traced. Pattern directions are given in step-by-step order.

MATERIALS
If you choose to make all 25 blocks for "Grandma's Last Quilt," you will need a total of 6 1/2 yards of bleached muslin for the background. A materials list for the appliqués accompanies each block pattern. Blanche used approximately 37 different prints and solids in her quilt.

You will also need assorted colors of embroidery floss to match some of the appliqué fabrics. Colors needed are listed in the block patterns.

To finish the quilt, you will need 5 yards of backing fabric, 3/4 yard of binding fabric and an 88" square of batting.

FABRICS
We suggest using 100% cotton. Wash fabric in warm water with mild detergent and no fabric softener. Wash darks separately and check for bleeding during the rinse cycle. If the color needs to be set, mix equal parts of white vinegar and table salt with water and soak the fabric in it. Dry fabric on a warm-to-hot setting to shrink it. Press with a hot dry iron to remove any wrinkles.

TOOLS
We recommend using appliqué pins to secure the pieces while stitching. Since appliqué pins are very short, your appliqué thread won't get caught as often or as easily as it would on longer pins.

It is important to use a very fine needle for appliqué. Sharps, or Milliners which are a bit longer than the Betweens used for quilting, are the best for needleturn appliqué. The higher the number, the finer the needle. We recommend a size 11 needle.

We also recommend using small embroidery, appliqué or tailor point scissors. Because they are sharp to the point, they allow you to make clean snips on "V's" and corners.

TEMPLATES
Place a sheet of clear template plastic or a piece of freezer paper (shiny side down) over the patterns and trace the cutting line(s) for each one. Cut them out on the lines. Use a permanent marker to record the pattern number on each template. Some pieces have design lines for reverse appliqué. Trace design lines onto the template(s). Using a razor knife, cut on the design lines.

MARKING FABRIC
Test marking tools for removability before using them. Sharpen pencils often. Place a piece of fine sandpaper beneath the fabric to prevent slipping, if desired.

Leaving at least a 3/8" space between them, trace around the plastic templates on the right side of the fabric. Press freezer paper templates, shiny side down, on the right side of the fabric to adhere them. Cut the pieces out, adding a 1/8" to 3/16" turn-under allowance. For reverse appliqué, trace the design lines of the areas that will be cut out, onto the fabric but don't cut them at this time.

NEEDLETURN APPLIQUÉ
To find the center of the block and create placement guidelines, fold the background square in quarters. Lightly press the folds. Open the background square and fold it in quarters diagonally. Press the folds. Pin the appliqué pieces to the background square in the order given in the directions, using the pressed lines as placement guides.

Using thread to match the appliqué piece, thread a needle with a 15" to 18" length and knot one end. Turn under the allowance and bring the needle from the wrong side of the background fabric up through the fold on the marked line of the appliqué piece. Push the needle through the background fabric, catching a few threads, and come back up through the appliqué piece on the marked line close to the first stitch. Use the point of the needle to smooth under the allowance and make another stitch in the same way. Continue needleturning and stitching until the piece is completely sewn to the background fabric. To reduce bulk, do not stitch where one appliqué piece will be overlapped by another.

REVERSE APPLIQUÉ
Reverse appliqué is done by trimming a shape from the interior of an appliqué piece. Trim 1/8" to 3/16" inside the marked line to allow for a turn under allowance. Needleturn the trimmed area to a background piece of fabric that has been placed right side up beneath the wrong side of the appliqué piece. The background fabric shows through the opening.

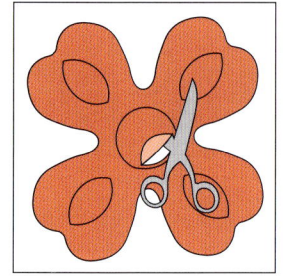

In some cases, the background fabric will be a small shape centered beneath the appliqué piece. To center the background shape you may find it helpful to hold the layers up to the light or to use a light box. After reverse appliquéing the appliqué piece to the shape, turn the unit over and trim the background shape 1/8" to 3/16" beyond the stitching.

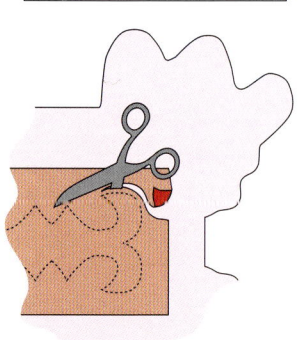

MAKING BIAS STRIPS
Cut the fabric for bias strips at a 45° angle. Cut 1"-wide strips, as shown.

Use one of the following 3 methods for making bias strips:

1. Press a 1"-wide bias strip in half lengthwise, right side out. Using a 1/4" seam allowance, stitch along the length to make a tube. Manipulate it so the seamline runs along the center of the tube. Press. Trim the seam allowance to 1/8" or if you wish to further reduce bulk, trim the seam

allowance off, including the stitching. This leaves a bias strip with both long edges turned under, ready for stitching.

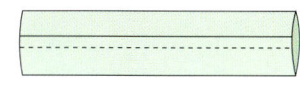

2. You may also use bias press bars. Press a 1"-wide bias strip in half lengthwise, right side out. Sew 1/4" from the fold. When you have sewn a few inches, test for accuracy by inserting a 1/4" metal Bias Bar™ into the sewn tube. It should fit snugly. Remove the Bias Bar, adjust your stitching if necessary, and continue sewing the bias strip to the end. Insert the 1/4" metal Bias Bar into the bias tube and trim the seam allowance to 1/8".

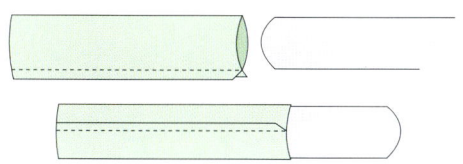

Move the seam to just shy of the center.

Using steam, lightly press the tube on both sides. Let the Bias Bar cool in the fabric before removing to ensure a flat, well-creased tube. Remove the Bias Bar when cool.

3. Cut a 3/4"-wide bias strip. Press the strip in thirds. Trim 1/8" from each long edge.

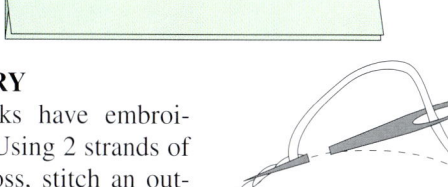

EMBROIDERY

Some blocks have embroidered details. Using 2 strands of embroidery floss, stitch an outline stitch, as shown.

MARKING QUILTING LINES

Mark the quilt top before basting the quilt together with the batting and backing. Use a very hard (#3 or #4) pencil or other marker. Test your marker first. Transfer paper designs by placing fabric over the design and tracing. Precut plastic stencils that fit the area you wish to quilt may be placed on top of the quilt and traced. Use a ruler to mark straight, even grids.

Outline quilting does not require marking. Simply eyeball 1/4" from the seam or stitch "in the ditch" next to the seam.

Masking tape can also be used to mark straight lines. Temporary quilting stencils can be made from clear adhesive-backed paper or freezer paper and reused many times. To avoid residue, do not leave tape or adhesive-backed paper on your quilt overnight.

BASTING

Cut the batting and backing at least 2" larger than the quilt top on all sides. Tape the backing, wrong side up, on a flat surface to anchor it. Smooth the batting on top, followed by the quilt top, right side up. Baste the three layers together to form a quilt sandwich. Begin at the center and baste horizontally, then vertically. Add more lines of basting approximately every 6" until the entire top is secured.

QUILTING

Quilting is done with a short, strong needle called a Between. The lower the number (size) of the needle, the larger it is. Begin with an 8 to 9 and progress to a 10 to 12. Use a thimble on the middle finger of the hand that pushes the needle. Begin quilting at the center of the quilt and work outward to keep the tension even and the quilting smooth.

Using an 18" length of quilting thread knotted at one end, insert the needle through the quilt top only and bring it up exactly where you will begin. Pop the knot through the fabric to bury it in the batting. Push the needle with the thimbled finger of the upper hand and slightly depress the fabric in front of the needle with the thumb. Redirect the needle back to the top of the quilt using the middle or index finger of the lower hand.

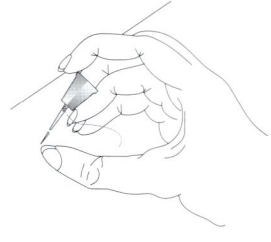

Repeat with each stitch, using a rocking motion. Finish by knotting the thread close to the surface and popping the knot through the fabric to bury it in the batting. Remove basting when all the quilting is done.

If you wish to machine quilt, we recommend consulting one of the many excellent books now available on the subject.

BINDING

Trim excess batting and backing to within 1/4" of the quilt top. Cut binding strips with the grain for straight-edge quilts. To make 1/2" finished binding, cut 2 1/2" wide strips. Sew strips together with diagonal seams; trim and press seams open.

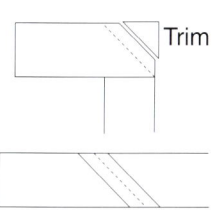

Fold the strip in half lengthwise, wrong side in, and press. Position the binding strip on the right side of the quilt top, aligning the raw edges of the binding with the edge of the quilt top. Leaving approximately 6" of the binding strip free and beginning several inches from one corner, stitch the binding to the quilt with a 1/2" seam allowance measured from the raw edge of the quilt back. When you reach a corner, stop stitching 1/2" from the edge and backstitch. Clip threads and remove the quilt from the machine. Fold the binding up and away from the quilt, forming a 45° angle as shown. Keeping the angled fold secure, fold the binding back down. This fold should be even with the edge of the quilt top. Beginning at the fold, stitch through all the layers.

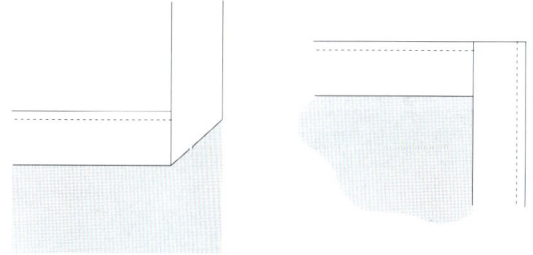

Continue stitching around the quilt in this manner to within 6" of the starting point. To finish, fold both strips back along the edge of the quilt so that the folded edges meet about 3" from both lines of stitching and the binding lies flat on the quilt. Finger press to crease the folds. Cut both strips 1 1/4" from the folds.

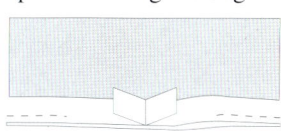

Open both strips and place the ends at right angles to each other, right sides together. Fold the bulk of the quilt out of your way. Join the strips with a diagonal seam as shown.

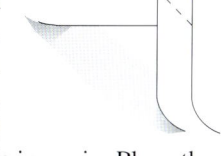

Trim the seam allowance to 1/4" and press it open. Fold the joined strip, wrong side in again. Place the binding flat against the quilt and finish stitching it to the quilt. Trim the layers as needed so that the binding edge will be filled with batting when you fold the binding to the back of the quilt.

Blindstitch the binding to the back, covering the seamline.

Remove visible markings. Sign and date your quilt.

"Grandma's Last Quilt" (83 1/2" square) by Blanche Burkett White

Row 1
Block A

Row 1
Block B

MATERIALS
- 17 1/2" square of bleached muslin for the background
- Pink print, at least 10" square
- Red with white polka dots, at least 9" x 12"
- Green solid at least 4 1/2" x 6"
- Dark green print, at least 7" square

CUTTING
- Cut 1: #1, pink print
- Cut 4: #2, red with white polka dots
- Cut 1: 3" x 5" rectangle, same red print
- Cut 4: 2 1/2"-long prepared bias strips, green solid
- Cut 8: #3, dark green print

DIRECTIONS
- Center the 3" x 5" red print rectangle, right side up, under the drawn center design of piece #1. Pin them together.
- Trimming as you stitch, reverse appliqué the #1 to the red print rectangle along the marked design line.
- Turn the unit wrong side up. Carefully trim the red print fabric 3/16" beyond the stitching.
- Center the prepared unit on the background square. Pin it in place.
- As you appliqué the unit to the square, tuck a 2 1/2" prepared bias strip under it at each corner. Refer to the block photo, as necessary.
- Pin a red print #2 to each corner of the background square, covering the remaining end of each bias strip and keeping the pieces at least 1" from the edges of the square. Trim the bias strips if necessary, leaving 3/16" to tuck under the #2 pieces. Pin the strips in place.
- Appliqué the strips to the background square.
- Appliqué the #2's.
- Referring to the block photo, pin and appliqué the dark green print #3's.
- Trim the block to 17" square, keeping the design centered.

MATERIALS
- 17 1/2" square of bleached muslin for the background
- Red check at least 2 3/4" square
- Green solid at least 5" x 9 1/2"
- Green print at least 6" x 8"
- Red floral at least 3 1/2" x 4"
- Red solid at least 8" x 12"

CUTTING
- Cut 1: #4, red check (without tracing the inner design line)
- Cut 4: 5 5/8"-long prepared bias strips, green solid
- Cut 4: #5, green print
- Cut 4: #6, red floral
- Cut 4: #7, red solid

DIRECTIONS
- Pin the red check #4 to the center of the background square.
- Referring to the block photo, tuck one end of each 5 5/8" prepared bias strip under the #4, placing the stems diagonally on the background square. Pin them in place.
- Remove the #4 piece. Appliqué the bias strips to the square.
- Appliqué the #4 to the center of the square, covering the ends of the strips.
- Appliqué the green print #5's between the bias strips, with the #5's touching the #4.
- Appliqué a red floral #6 to each corner of the block, covering the remaining end of each bias strip.
- Pin the red solid #7's to the background square, leaving a 1/4" space between the #6 and #7 pieces and keeping the pieces at least 1" from the edges of the square. Refer to the block photo, as necessary.
- Appliqué the #7's to the background square.
- Trim the block to 17" square, keeping the design centered.

Row 1
Block C

Row 1
Block D

MATERIALS
- 17 1/2" square of bleached muslin for the background
- Red print, at least 9" x 11"
- Red solid, at least 2 1/4" x 4 1/2"
- Dark green solid at least 12" x 18"

CUTTING
- Cut 4: #8, red print
- Cut 2: #9, red print
- Cut 2: #10 red solid
- Cut 8: #3, dark green solid
- Cut 2: 7 3/4"-long prepared bias strips, dark green solid
- Cut 2: 6 1/4"-long prepared bias strips, dark green solid

DIRECTIONS
- Referring to the block photo, pin a dark green solid #3 to one corner of the background square, diagonally, keeping it 1 1/4" from the edges of the square. Appliqué the #3 to the square. Appliqué a dark green solid #3 to the opposite corner in the same manner.
- Pin the 7 3/4" prepared bias strips to the background square in a curve, as shown.
- Pin the red print #8's to the background square, covering the ends of the bias strips and keeping the #8's at least 1 1/4" from the edges of the square.
- Pin the 6 1/4" prepared bias strips to the background square in a curve, as shown, tucking the ends under the #8 pieces.
- Pin the red print #9's and red solid #10's to the square, covering the remaining ends of the bias strips.
- Rearrange the pieces as necessary.
- Appliqué the bias strips to the square.
- Appliqué the remaining pieces in the following order: red print #8's, red print #9's, red solid #10's and dark green solid #3's. Refer to the block photo, as necessary.
- Trim the block to 17" square, keeping the design centered.

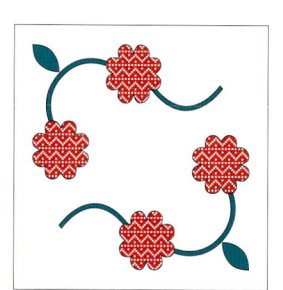

MATERIALS
- 17 1/2" square of bleached muslin for the background
- Red print, at least 11" x 16"
- Bleached muslin, at least 10" square
- Red solid, at least 5 1/2" square
- Light green print, at least 9" square

CUTTING
- Cut 1: 10" square, red print
- Cut 4: #12, red print
- Cut 4: #12R, red print
- Cut 1: #11, bleached muslin
- Cut 1: #4, bleached muslin (without tracing the inner design line)
- Cut 4: #13, red solid
- Cut 8: #3, light green print
- Cut 4: 2 3/4"-long prepared bias strips, light green print

DIRECTIONS
- Center and pin the bleached muslin #11 on the right side of the 10" red print square. Appliqué the outside edge of the #11 to the square.
- Trimming as you stitch, reverse appliqué the center of the #11 to the square along the marked circle. Center the bleached muslin #4 in the center of the circle. Appliqué the #4 to the red print square.

- Center and pin the prepared center unit on the background square.
- Referring to the block photo, pin the 2 3/4" prepared bias strips to the corners of the square, tucking one end of each stem under the prepared unit.

(continued on page 11)

Row 1
Block E

Row 2
Block F

MATERIALS
- 17 1/2" square of bleached muslin for the background
- Red print, at least 9" x 11"
- Red with white polka dots, at least 4" x 6"
- Dark green print, at least 14" square

CUTTING
- Cut 4: #14, red print
- Cut 2: #12, red print
- Cut 4: #15, red with white polka dots
- Cut 8: #16, dark green print
- Cut 4: 8"-long prepared bias strips, dark green print

DIRECTIONS
- Referring to the block photo, lay the 8" prepared bias strips on the background square. Place the red print #14's and polka dot #15's on the square followed by the dark green print #16's and the red print #12's.
- Rearrange the pieces, as desired, keeping them at least 1 1/4" from the edges of the square. Pin the pieces in place.
- Appliqué the pieces in the following order: dark green print #16's, dark green print bias strips, red print #14's, polka dot #15's and red print #12's.
- Trim the block to 17" square, keeping the design centered.

MATERIALS
- 17 1/2" square of bleached muslin for the background
- Green solid, at least 18" square
- Green stripe, at least 11" square
- Red solid, at least 8" square
- Green embroidery floss

CUTTING
- Cut 2: 22"-long prepared bias strips, green solid
- Cut 8: #18, green stripe (Refer to the block photo for placement of the stripe.)
- Cut 32: #17, red solid

DIRECTIONS
- Referring to the block photo, pin the 22" prepared bias strips to the background square, crossing them in the center of the square and keeping the ends at least 1 1/4" from the edge of the square. Pin them in place.
- Pin the green stripe #18's to the square, keeping them at least 1 1/2" from the edges of the square. Reposition the #18's as necessary to make room for the grape clusters.
- Using a pencil, lightly trace the grape cluster Placement Diagram 4 times on the background square. NOTE: *Trace just inside the lines so the pencil marks will be covered by the appliqué pieces.*
- Appliqué the pieces in the following order: green bias strips, green stripe #18's and red solid #17's.
- Using 2 strands of green embroidery floss and an outline stitch, embroider a stem connecting each #18 to the adjacent bias strip. Embroider a stem connecting each grape cluster to the adjacent bias strip and a tendril near the base of each stem.

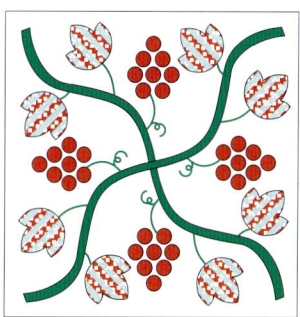

- Trim the block to 17" square, keeping the design centered.

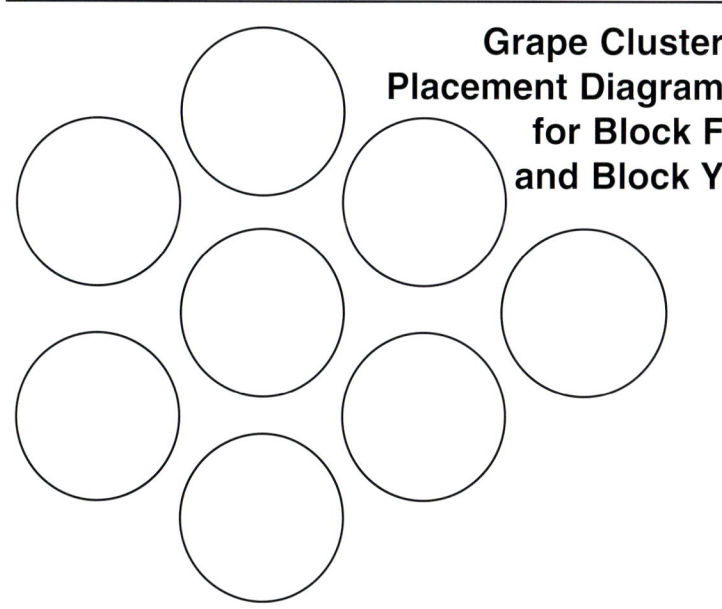

Grape Cluster Placement Diagram for Block F and Block Y

Row 2
Block G

Row 2
Block H

MATERIALS
- 17 1/2" square of bleached muslin for the background
- Red solid, at least 16" square
- Dark green solid, at least 11" x 16"

CUTTING
- Cut 12: #19, red solid
- Cut 8: #20, dark green solid
- Cut 4: 4 3/4"-long prepared bias strips, dark green solid
- Cut 4: 3 1/4"-long prepared bias strips, dark green solid

DIRECTIONS
- Fold each 4 3/4" prepared bias strip in half to find the center. Center one of the strips on a diagonal crease of the background square. Appliqué the strip to the square. NOTE: *We recommend trimming off the seam allowance on the wrong side of these bias strips because of the bulk created in the center where they cross each other.*
- Center and appliqué a bias strip to the square on the remaining diagonal crease in the same manner, crossing the first strip.
- In the same manner, appliqué a bias strip horizontally, then appliqué the remaining 4 3/4" bias strip vertically.
- Appliqué 4 red solid #19's, covering the ends of the horizontal and vertical bias strips.
- Pin 4 red solid #19's to the background square, covering the ends of the diagonal bias strips.
- Referring to the block photo, tuck a 3 1/4" prepared bias strip under each pinned #19.
- Pin the remaining #19's to the background square, covering the remaining ends of the 3 1/4" bias strips. Pin the dark green solid #20's to the square.
- Rearrange the pieces as desired, keeping them at least 1" from the edges of the square.
- Appliqué the pieces in the following order: 3 1/4" bias strips, red solid #19's and dark green solid #20's.
- Trim the block to 17" square, keeping the design centered.

MATERIALS
- 17 1/2" square of bleached muslin for the background
- Green print, at least 11" x 14 1/2"
- Green solid, at least 5" x 7"
- Red with white polka dots, at least 9" x 11"
- Red solid, at least 4" x 5"

CUTTING
- Cut 1: #21, green print NOTE: *Trace around the plastic or freezer paper template and cut the shape out 1/2" beyond the traced line.*
- Cut 8: #23, green print
- Cut 4: 2 3/4"-long prepared bias strips, green solid
- Cut 4: #8, red with white polka dots
- Cut 1: 1 1/2" square, red with white polka dots
- Cut 8: #22, red solid

DIRECTIONS
- Center and pin the 1 1/2" polka dot square, right side up, under the marked square on the green print #21.
- Trimming as you stitch, reverse appliqué the #21 to the square along the marked design line.
- Center and pin a red solid #22, right side up, under each of the remaining inner design lines on piece #21. Reverse appliqué the #21 to the #22's along the marked lines.
- Trim the outer edge of the #21, leaving a 1/8" to 3/16" turn under allowance.
- Center the #21 right side up on the background square, placing the shorter petals diagonally on the square. Pin it in place.
- Tuck one end of a 2 3/4" prepared bias strip under each diagonal petal. Pin them in place. Appliqué the bias strips to the square.
- Appliqué the outer edge of the #21 to the square.
- Appliqué a polka dot #8 to each corner of the background square, covering the ends of the bias strips and keeping the #8's 1 1/4" from the edges of the square.
- Referring to the block photo, appliqué the green print #23's to the background square.
- Trim the block to 17" square, keeping the design centered.

Row 2
Block I

Row 2
Block J

MATERIALS
- 17 1/2" square of bleached muslin for the background
- Red print, at least 13" square
- Red solid, at least 4 1/2" x 6"
- Dark green stripe, at least 9" x 12"
- Red embroidery floss

CUTTING
- Cut 1: #24, red print (Fold the square in quarters. Place the #24 on the folds as indicated.)
- Cut 12: #17, red solid
- Cut 4: #25, dark green stripe

DIRECTIONS
- Center the red print #24 on the background square. Pin it in place.
- Referring to the block photo, tuck the dark green stripe #25's under the #24. Pin them in place.
- Appliqué the #25's.
- Appliqué the outside edge of the #24.
- Trimming as you stitch, reverse appliqué the #24 to the background square along the marked circle.
- Referring to the block photo, appliqué the #17's to the background square.
- Usng red embroidery floss and an outline stitch, embroider a stem connecting each #17 to the #24.
- Trim the block to 17" square, keeping the design centered.

MATERIALS
- 17 1/2" square of bleached muslin for the background
- Red print, at least 9" x 11"
- Light green solid, at least 9 1/2" x 13"

CUTTING
- Cut 1: #26, red print
- Cut 4: #3, red print
- Cut 4: #27, red print
- Cut 4: #16, light green solid
- Cut 4: 5 1/2"-long prepared bias strips, light green solid

DIRECTIONS
- Referring to the block photo, center the red print #26 on the background square. Pin the 5 1/2" prepared bias strips to the square, tucking one end of each under the #26.
- Tuck the stem of each light green solid #16 under a bias strip. Pin the #16's in place.
- Appliqué the #16's to the background square.
- Appliqué the bias strips.
- Appliqué the remaining pieces in the following order: red print #26; red print #27's, covering the ends of the bias strips and keeping them at least 1 1/8" from the edges of the square; and the red print #3's.
- Trim the block to 17" square, keeping the design centered.

Row 1
Block D
(continued from page 8)

- Pin the red solid #13's to the background square, covering the remaining ends of the bias strips and keeping them at least 1" from the edges of the square. Pin the light green print #3's to the square, keeping the pieces at least 1" from the edges of the square.
- Pin the red print #12's and #12R's to the background square, keeping them 1 1/2" from the edges.
- Rearrange the pieces as necessary.
- Appliqué the bias strips.
- Appliqué the center unit to the background square.
- Appliqué the remaining pieces in the following order: red solid #13's, light green #3's and red print #12's and #12R's.
- Trim the block to 17" square, keeping the design centered.

Row 3
Block K

Row 3
Block L

MATERIALS
- 17 1/2" square of bleached muslin for the background
- Green print, at least 18" square
- Yellow print, at least 10 1/2" x 12"
- Green embroidery floss

CUTTING
- Cut 1: 25"-long prepared bias strip, green print
- Cut 12: #3, green print
- Cut 8: #28, yellow print

DIRECTIONS
- Measuring 4" from the center of the background square, make light pencil marks in an arc. Connect the marks to make a circle.

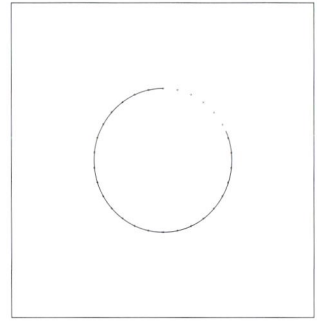

- Open the pressed edges of the 25" prepared bias strip. Sew the ends of the strip together to form a ring. Finger press the seam open.
- Refold the pressed edges and appliqué the bias ring to the background square, covering the drawn circle.
- Pin four yellow print #28's to the background square, outside the bias ring along the vertical and horizontal folds, placing them 1/4" away from the bias ring. Appliqué them in place.
- Appliqué the remaining #28's to the square along the diagonal folds, placing them 5/8" away from the bias ring.
- Referring to the block photo, appliqué the green print #3's to the background square.
- Using 2 strands of green embroidery floss and an outline stitch, embroider a stem connecting each #28 to the bias ring.
- Trim the block to 17" square, keeping the design centered.

MATERIALS
- 17 1/2" square of bleached muslin for the background
- Light green print, at least 18" square
- Red solid, at least 8" square

CUTTING
- Cut 1: 25"-long prepared bias strip, light green print
- Cut 4: 3 1/2"-long prepared bias strips, light green print
- Cut 12: #29, light green print
- Cut 4: #19, red solid
- Cut 12: #17, red solid

DIRECTIONS
- Measuring 4" from the center of the background square, make light pencil marks in an arc. Connect the marks to make a circle.

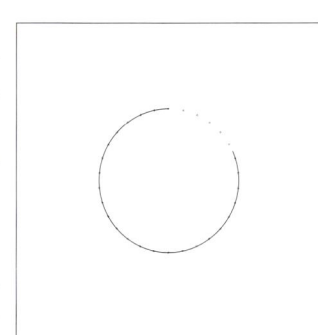

- Referring to the block photo, place one end of each 3 1/2" prepared bias strip on the background square, slightly overlapping the drawn circle. Curve the strips toward the corners of the square.
- Appliqué the 3 1/2" bias strips to the background square.
- Open the pressed edges of the 25" prepared bias strip. Sew the ends of the strip together to form a ring. Finger press the seam open.
- Refold the pressed edges and appliqué the bias ring to the square, covering the drawn circle and the ends of the 3 1/2" bias strips.
- Appliqué the red solid #19's to the square, covering the remaining ends of the bias strips and keeping them at least 1 1/4" from the edges of the square.
- Referring to the block photo, pin 3 light green print #29's and a red solid #17 between 2 appliquéd bias strips, along the outside edge of the bias ring. Appliqué them to the background square.
- Appliqué green print #29's and red solid #17's between the remaining green print bias strips in the same manner.
- Appliqué the remaining red solid #17's to the background square along the inside edge of the bias ring.
- Trim the block to 17" square, keeping the design centered.

Row 3
Block M

Row 3
Block N

MATERIALS
- 17 1/2" square of bleached muslin for the background
- Red solid, at least 12" square
- Red print, at least 7" x 10"
- Green print, at least 3 1/2" x 6 1/2"
- Green solid, at least 6 1/2" x 8"

CUTTING
- Cut 16: #30, red solid
- Cut 1: #31, red solid
- Cut 4: #2, red print
- Cut 4: #3, green print
- Cut 4: 4"-long prepared bias strips, green solid

DIRECTIONS
- Using a pencil, trace the Placement Diagram (shown on page 32) on one quarter of the background square, as shown. Trace just inside the design lines so the marks will be covered by the appliqué pieces.
- Trace the design on the remaining quarters of the background square in the same manner.
- Referring to the block photo, pin a red print #2 to each corner of the background square, keeping them 1 5/8" from the edges of the square.
- Lay a 4" prepared bias strip on the background square, curving it toward one corner. Place it so one end overlaps the drawn design line by about 1/8" and the other end tucks under the adjacent red print #2.
- Appliqué the bias strip in place. Appliqué the remaining bias strips in the same manner.
- Appliqué the red print #30's, covering the design lines.
- Appliqué the red solid #31 in the center.
- Appliqué the red print #2's in place.
- Appliqué the green print #3's to the background square, referring to the block photo for placement.
- Trim the block to 17" square, keeping the design centered.

MATERIALS
- 17 1/2" square of bleached muslin for the background
- Green solid at least 13" square
- Red solid at least 10 1/2" square
- Red embroidery floss

CUTTING
- Cut 1: #4, green solid
- Cut 8: #32, green solid
- Cut 8: #6, red solid

DIRECTIONS
- Center and pin the green solid #4 to the background square.
- Appliqué the outer edge of the #4.
- Trimming as you stitch, reverse appliqué the #4 along the marked inner circle to form a ring, as shown.
- Referring to the block photo, pin the green solid #32's to the background square, placing them about 1/8" from the center ring.
- Appliqué the #32's.
- Appliqué the red solid #6's between the #32's.
- Using 2 strands of red embroidery floss and an outline stitch, embroider a stem connecting each #6 to the inner point of an adjacent #32.
- Trim the block to 17" square, keeping the design centered.

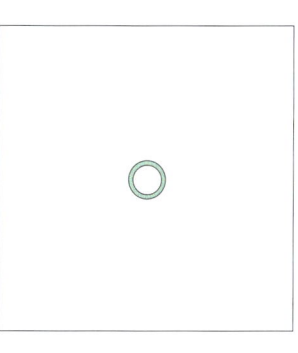

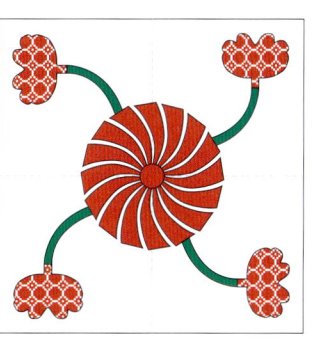

Row 3
Block O

Row 4
Block P

MATERIALS
- 17 1/2" square of bleached muslin for the background
- Red print at least 9" square
- Red solid at least 6" square
- Green print at least 10" x 16"

CUTTING
- Cut 1: #33, red print
- Cut 16: #17 red solid
- Cut 4: #34, green print

DIRECTIONS
- Center the red print #33 on the background square, as shown. Appliqué the outer edges.

- Trimming as you stitch, reverse appliqué the #33 along the inner design lines.
- Referring to the block photo, appliqué a green print #34 in each corner of the background square, keeping them at least 2" from the edges of the square.
- Appliqué the red solid #17's to the background square.
- Trim the block to 17" square, keeping the design centered.

MATERIALS
- 17 1/2" square of bleached muslin for the background
- Green solid, at least 18" square
- Green print, at least 9" x 10 1/2"
- Red with white polka dots, at least 10" square

CUTTING
- Cut 1: 23 1/2"-long prepared bias strip, green solid
- Cut 4: 3 3/4"-long prepared bias strips, green solid
- Cut 6: #37, green print
- Cut 6: #3, green print
- Cut 4: #35, red with white polka dots
- Cut 6: #36, red with white polka dots

DIRECTIONS
- Measuring 3 3/4" from the center of the background square, make light pencil marks in an arc. Connect the marks to make a circle.
- Referring to the block photo, place one end of each 3 3/4" prepared bias strip on the background square, slightly overlapping the drawn circle. Curve the strips toward the corners of the square.
- Appliqué the 3 3/4" bias strips to the square.
- Open the pressed edges of the 23 1/2" prepared bias strip. Sew the ends of the strip together to form a ring. Finger press the seam open.
- Refold the pressed edges and appliqué the bias ring to the background square, covering the drawn circle and the ends of the 3 3/4" bias strips.
- Referring to the block photo, place the green print #37's on the background square. Tuck a polka dot #36 under each #37. Pin the pieces to the square.
- Appliqué the pieces in place.
- Appliqué a polka dot #35 to each corner of the background square, keeping them at least 1" from the edges of the square and covering the ends of the bias strips.
- Appliqué the green print #3's to the background square.
- Trim the block to 17" square, keeping the design centered.

Row 4 Block Q

MATERIALS
- 17 1/2" square of bleached muslin for the background
- Red solid, at least 14" square
- Green print, at least 9" x 14"

CUTTING
- Cut 1: #38, red solid
- Cut 4: #39, red solid
- Cut 4: #40, green print

DIRECTIONS
- With a 1/4" seam allowance, sew the green print #40's to the red solid #38, as shown.

- Referring to the block photo, center the unit on the background square and pin it in place.
- Tuck the ends of the red solid #39's under the unit and pin them to the square.
- Appliqué the red solid #39's.
- Appliqué the outside edges of the center unit.
- Trimming as you stitch, reverse appliqué the center of the #38 along the square design line.
- Trim the block to 17" square, keeping the design centered.

Row 4 Block R

MATERIALS
- 17 1/2" square of bleached muslin for the background
- Red solid, at least 13" square
- Green print, at least 10" x 14"
- Green solid, at least 5" x 6 1/2"

CUTTING
- Cut 1: #41, red solid (without tracing the inner design lines)
- Cut 4: #42, red solid
- Cut 4: #43, red solid
- Cut 4: 6"-long prepared bias strips, green print
- Cut 1: #41, green print
- Cut 4: #3, green print
- Cut 4: #44, green solid

DIRECTIONS
- Place the right side of the red solid #41 against the wrong side of the green print #41, aligning the raw edge. Pin them together.
- Trimming as you stitch, reverse appliqué the green print #41 seed shapes and the center circle along the design lines.
- Turn the unit over and carefully trim the excess red solid fabric away about 1/4" beyond the stitching.
- Referring to the block photo, pin the center unit to the background square.
- Tuck one end of each 6" prepared bias strip under the center unit. Pin them to the background square, curving them toward the corners.
- Pin a red solid #42 to each corner of the background square, covering the ends of the bias strips and keeping them at least 1" from the edges of the square.
- Appliqué the bias strips.
- Appliqué the center unit.
- Appliqué the remaining pieces in the following order: outer edges of the red solid #42's, green print #3's, red solid #43's and green solid #44's.
- Trimming as you stitch, reverse appliqué the center circle of each red solid #42.
- Trim the block to 17" square, keeping the design centered.

Row 4
Block S

Row 4
Block T

MATERIALS
- 17 1/2" square of bleached muslin for the background
- Red solid, at least 10" square
- Red print, at least 8" square
- Red with white polka dots, at least 6" x 8"
- Dark green solid, at least 9" x 12"

CUTTING
- Cut 1: #1, red solid
- Cut 4: #47, red print
- Cut 2: #45, red with white polka dots
- Cut 4: #46, red with white polka dots
- Cut 4: 2 1/4"-long prepared bias strips, dark green solid
- Cut 16: #3, dark green solid

DIRECTIONS
- Center the red solid #1 on the background square. Pin it in place.
- Referring to the block photo, tuck one end of each 2 1/4" prepared bias strip under the #1. Pin them to the background square.
- Appliqué the dark green bias strips.
- Appliqué the outer edge of the #1.
- Trimming as you stitch, reverse appliqué the #1 along the inner design lines.
- Pin a red print #47 to each corner of the square, covering the ends of the bias strips and keeping the #47's at least 1 1/4" from the edges of the square.
- Tuck a polka dot #46 under each #47.
- Working on one corner at a time, appliqué the #46 then the #47.
- Appliqué the polka dot #45's.
- Appliqué the dark green solid #3's.
- Trim the block to 17" square, keeping the design centered.

MATERIALS
- 17 1/2" square of bleached muslin for the background
- Red print, at least 8 1/2" square
- Aqua print, at least 13" square
- Yellow print, at least 8" square
- Aqua embroidery floss

CUTTING
- Cut 1: #48, red print
- Cut 4: #49, aqua print
- Cut 4: #19, yellow print

DIRECTIONS
- Center and pin the red print #48 to the background square.
- Appliqué the outer edge of the #48.
- Trimming as you stitch, reverse appliqué the #48 along the inner design lines.
- Referring to the block photo, pin the aqua print #49's to the corners of the background square with the stem end touching the #48.
- Appliqué the #49's.
- Appliqué the yellow print #19's between the #49's, placing them 1/2" from the red print #48.
- Using 2 strands of aqua embroidery floss and an outline stitch, embroider a stem connecting each #19 to the #48.
- Trim the block to 17" square, keeping the design centered.

Row 5
Block U

Row 5
Block V

MATERIALS
- 17 1/2" square of bleached muslin for the background
- Red solid, at least 10" x 13"
- Dark green solid, at least 10" square
- Yellow print, at least 3 1/2" x 5 1/2"

CUTTING
- Cut 1: #50, red solid
- Cut 4: #52, red solid
- Cut 4: 4"-long prepared bias strips, dark green solid
- Cut 12: #53, dark green solid
- Cut 1: #51, yellow print
- Cut 4: #31, yellow print

DIRECTIONS
- Center the red solid #50 on the background square. Pin it in place.
- Referring to the block photo, tuck one end of each 4" prepared bias strip under the #50. Appliqué the strips.
- Appliqué the #50.
- Appliqué a red solid #52 in each corner of the block, covering the ends of the bias strips.
- Appliqué the yellow print #51 to the center of the #50.
- Appliqué the yellow print #31's to the #52's, referring to the block photo for placement.
- Appliqué the dark green #53's.
- Trim the block to 17" square, keeping the design centered.

MATERIALS
- 17 1/2" square of bleached muslin for the background
- Light green print, at least 10" x 14"
- Light green solid, at least 7" square
- Red solid, at least 4 1/2" square
- Red print, at least 7" x 10" square

CUTTING
- Cut 1: #54, light green print
- Cut 2: #37, light green print
- Cut 4: 6 1/2"-long prepared bias strips, light green print
- Cut 8: #3, light green solid
- Cut 2: #36, red solid
- Cut 4: #17, red solid
- Cut 4: #2, red print

DIRECTIONS
- Center the light green print #54 on the background square. Pin it in place.
- Referring to the block photo, tuck one end of each 6 1/2" prepared bias strip under the #54. Curve the strips toward the corners of the block. Pin them in place.
- Appliqué the bias strips.
- Appliqué the #54 to the background square along the outer edge.
- Trimming as you stitch, reverse appliqué the #54 along the inner circle design line.
- Referring to the block photo, pin the red solid #36's and light green print #37's inside the circle.
- Appliqué the #36's.
- Appliqué the #37's.
- Pin a red print #2 to each corner of the background square, covering the ends of the bias strips and keeping the #2's at least 1 1/4" from the edges of the square. Appliqué them in place.
- Appliqué a red solid #17 beside each bias strip, keeping them 1/8" away from the light green print circle and 1/8" from the bias strips.
- Appliqué the light green solid #3's.
- Trim the block to 17" square, keeping the design centered.

Row 5
Block W

Row 5
Block X

MATERIALS
- 17 1/2" square of bleached muslin for the background
- Dark green solid, at least 14" square
- Red with white polka dots, at least 6" square
- Yellow print, at least 13" square
- Dark green embroidery floss

CUTTING
- Cut 1: 18 1/2"-long prepared bias strip, dark green solid
- Cut 4: 4"-long prepared bias strips, dark green solid
- Cut 4: #56, dark green solid
- Cut 1: #55, red with white polka dots
- Cut 8: #27, yellow print

DIRECTIONS
- Measuring 3" from the center of the background square, make light pencil marks in an arc. Connect the marks to make a circle.

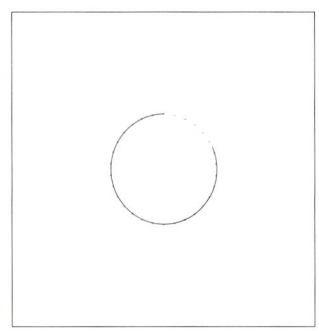

- Referring to the block photo, place one end of each 4" prepared bias strip on the background square, slightly overlapping the drawn circle. Curve the strips toward the corners of the square.
- Appliqué the 4" bias strips to the square.
- Open the pressed edges of the 18 1/2" prepared bias strip. Sew the ends together to form a ring. Finger press the seam open.
- Refold the pressed edges and appliqué the bias ring to the background square, covering the drawn circle and the ends of the 4" bias strips.
- Referring to the block photo, center and pin the polka dot #55 to the background square, overlapping the dark green bias ring.

MATERIALS
- 17 1/2" square of bleached muslin for the background
- Red print, at least 13" square
- Green print, at least 9" square
- Red solid, at least 8" x 10"

CUTTING
- Cut 1: #57, red print
- Cut 8: #58, green print
- Cut 4: #2, red solid

DIRECTIONS
- Center and pin the red print #57 to the background square. Appliqué the outer edge.
- Trimming as you stitch, reverse appliqué the #57 along the inner design lines.
- Referring to the block photo, pin 2 green print #58's and a red solid #2 to each corner of the background square. Keep the tips of the #58's at least 1" from the edges of the square.
- Appliqué the #58's and #2's.
- Trim the block to 17" square, keeping the design centered.

- Appliqué the outer edge of the #55 to the square.
- Trimming as you stitch, reverse appliqué the center circle along the design line.
- Referring to the block photo, pin a yellow print #27 to each corner of the background square, covering the ends of the 4" bias strips. Appliqué the #27's to the square.
- Pin a dark green solid #56 beside each bias strip, keeping the point about 1/4" away from the bias ring. Appliqué them to the square.
- Pin and appliqué the remaining yellow print #27's to the background square, referring to the block photo for placement.
- Using 2 strands of dark green embroidery floss and an outline stitch, embroider a stem connecting the last four #27's to the dark green #56's.
- Trim the block to 17" square, keeping the design centered.

Row 5
Block Y

Full-Size Appliqué Patterns for Grandma's Last Quilt

(continued on pages 20-32)

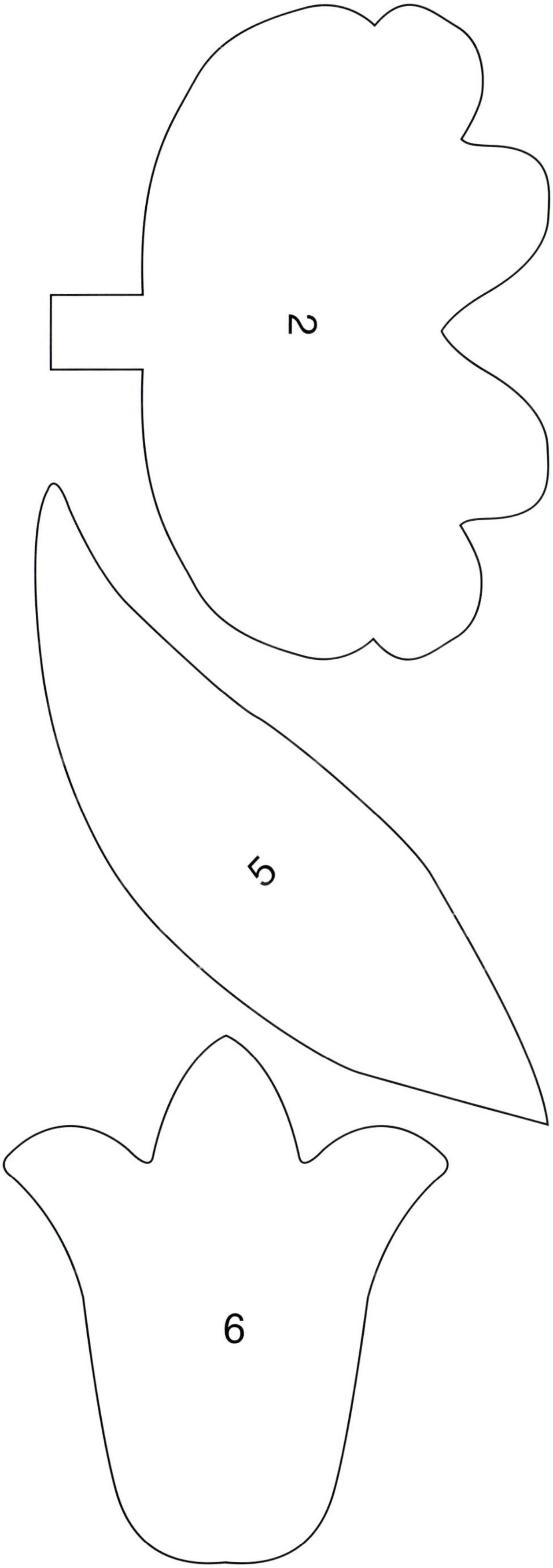

MATERIALS
- 17 1/2" square of bleached muslin for the background
- Green stripe, at least 11" square
- Dark green solid, at least 11" square
- Red solid, at least 9" square

CUTTING
- Cut 8: #18, green stripe (Refer to the block photo for placement of the stripe)
- Cut 8: 5 1/2"-long prepared bias strips, dark green solid
- Cut 32: #17, red solid

DIRECTIONS
- Using a pencil, lightly trace the grape cluster Placement Diagram on page 9 on the background square, keeping the grape at the outer point of the cluster 2" from the edge of the square. NOTE: *Trace just inside the design lines so the pencil marks will be covered by the appliqué pieces. Trace the design 3 more times in the same manner.*

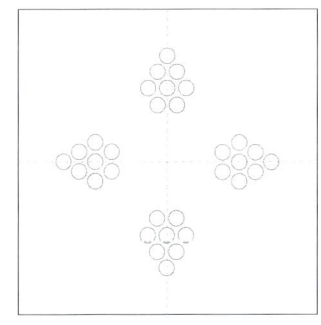

- Referring to the block photo, place 2 green stripe #18's in one corner of the square keeping them at least 1" from the edges of the square. Pin them in place. 
- Lay two 5 1/2" prepared bias strips on the square, tucking one end of each strip under a #18 and the other end overlapping a drawn grape by about 1/8". Gently curve the strips and cross one over the other, as shown.

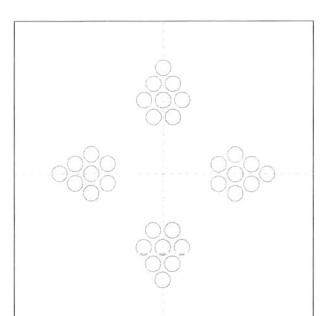

- Appliqué the bias strips.
- In the same manner, appliqué the remaining bias strips.
- Appliqué the #18's.
- Appliqué the red solid #17's.
- Trim the block to 17" square, keeping the design centered.

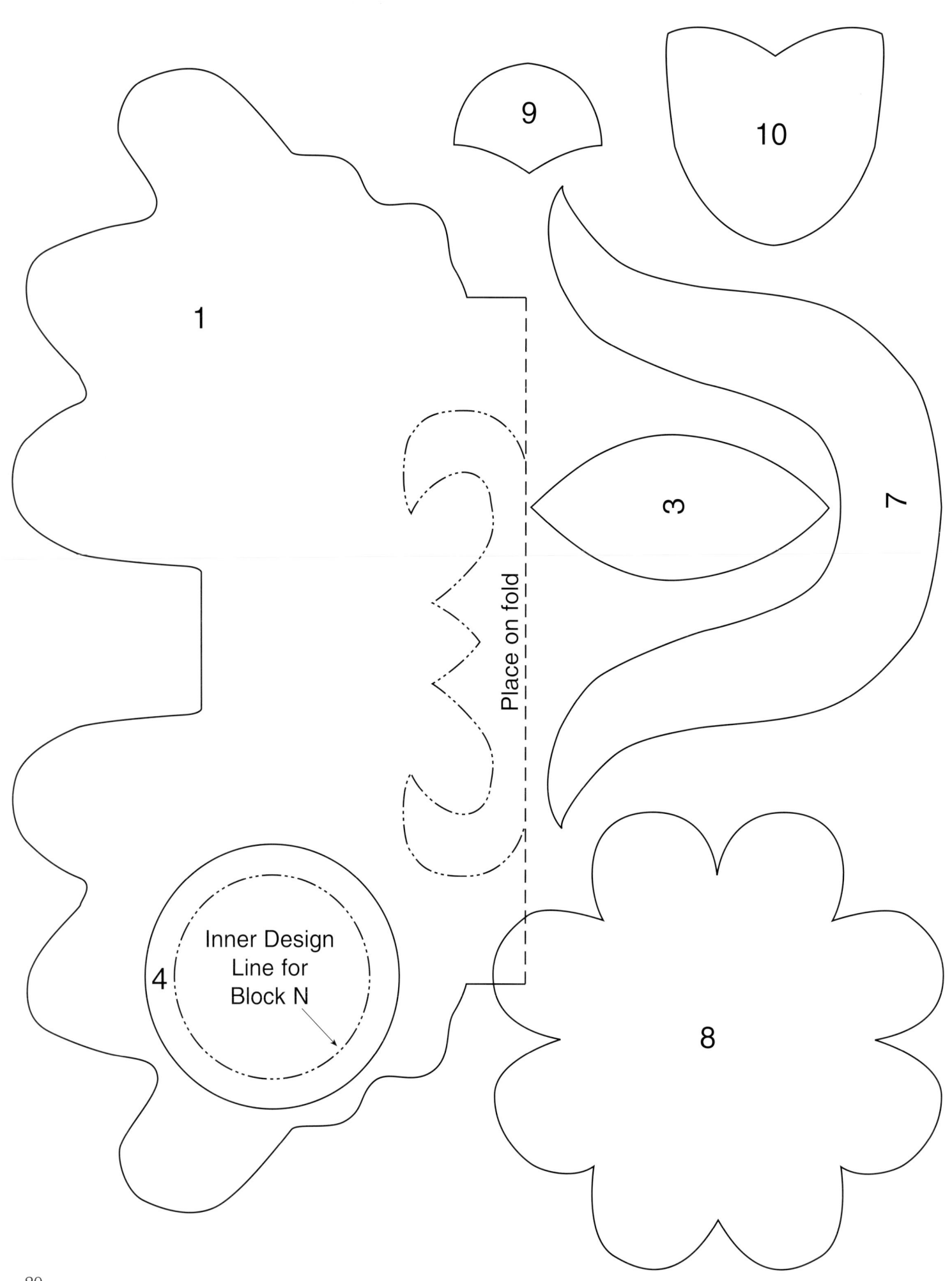

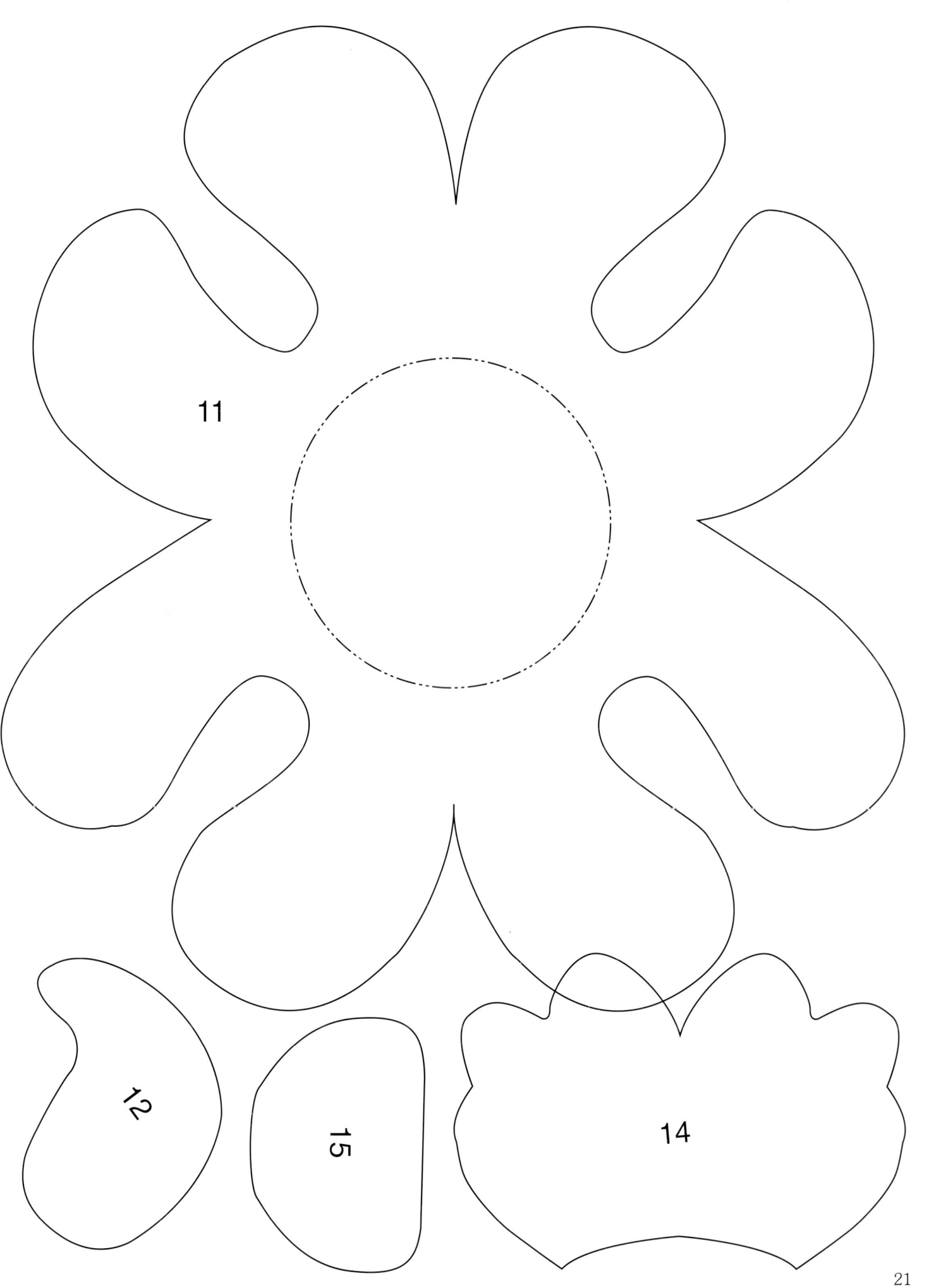

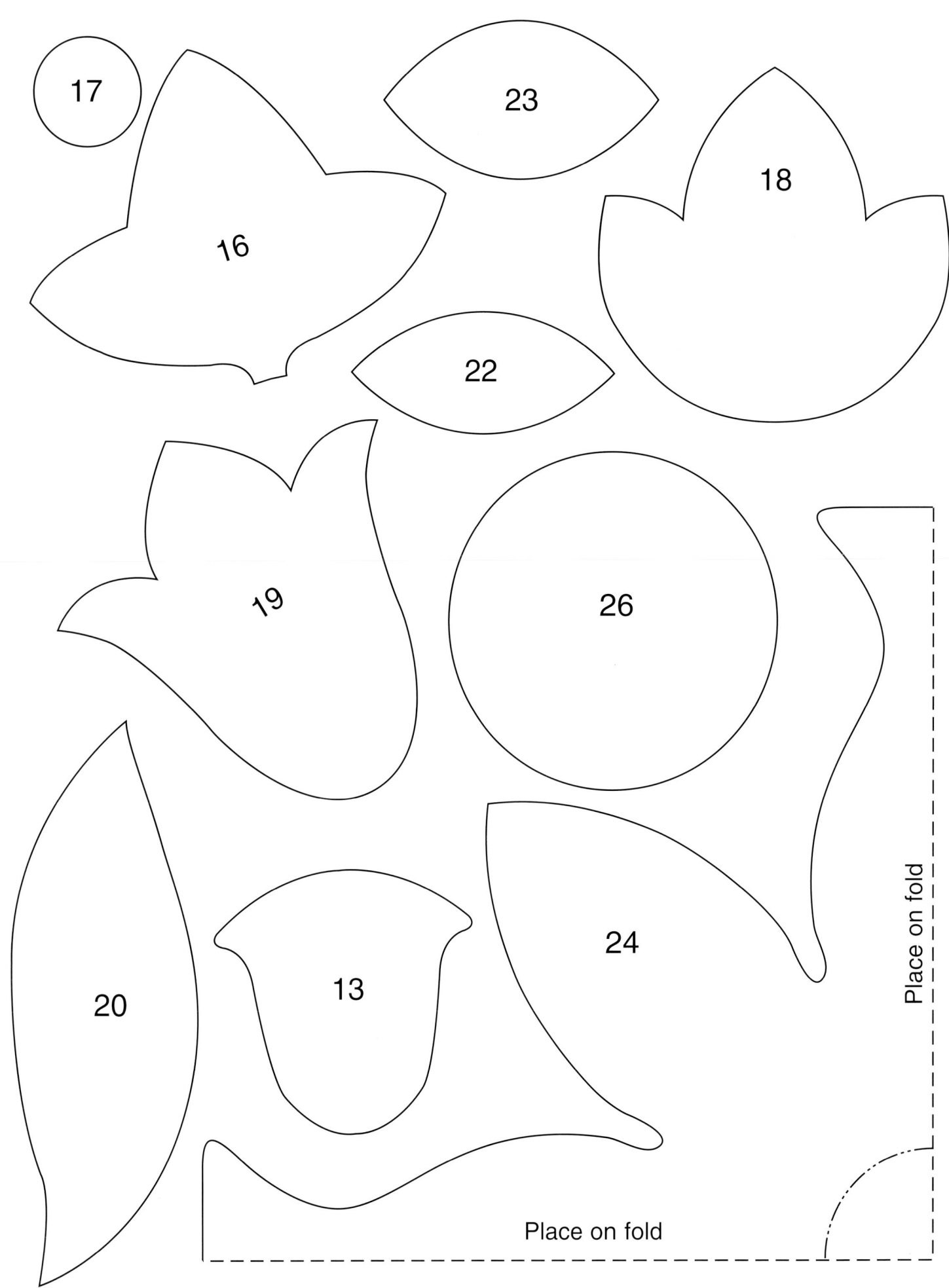

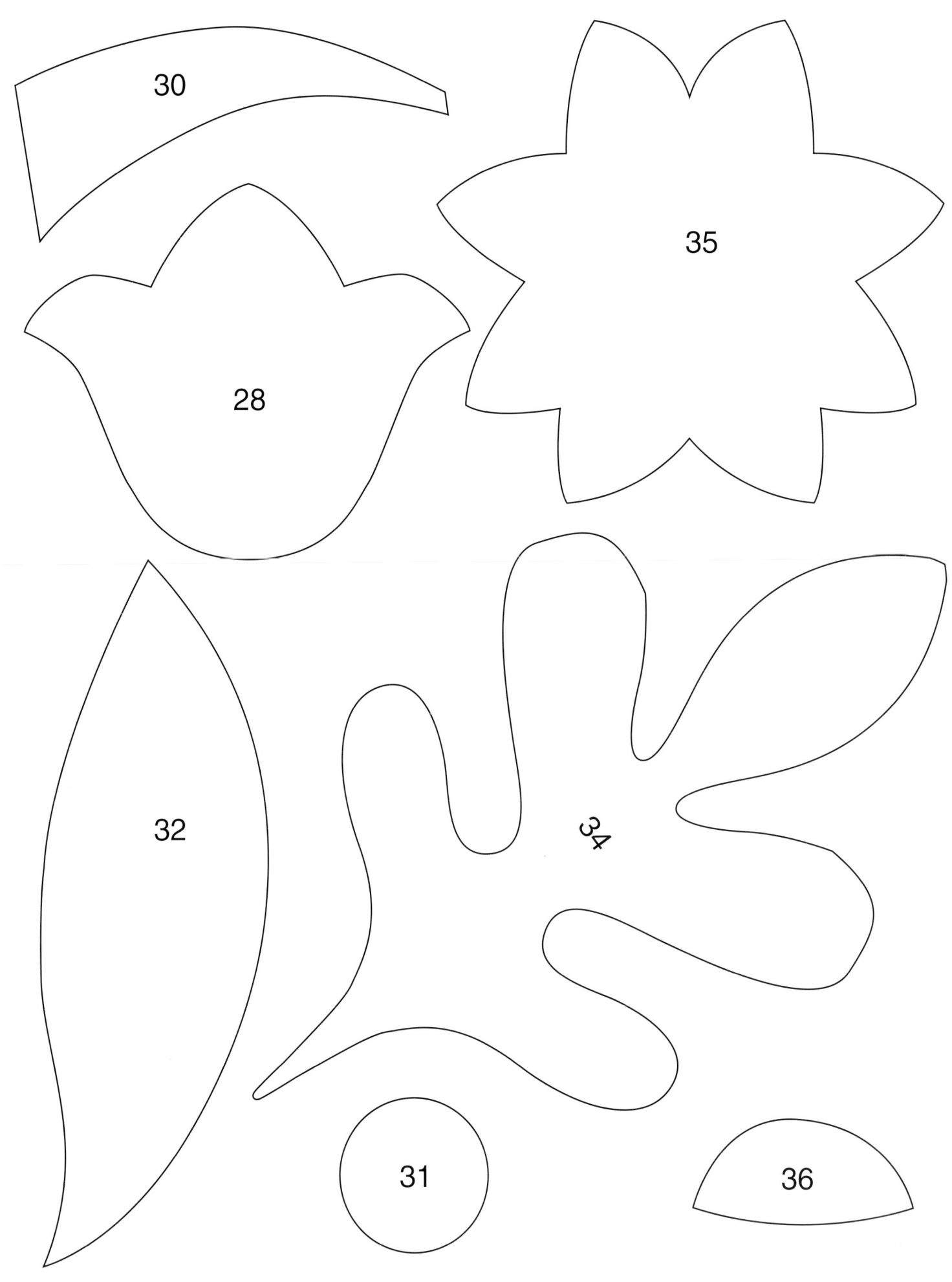

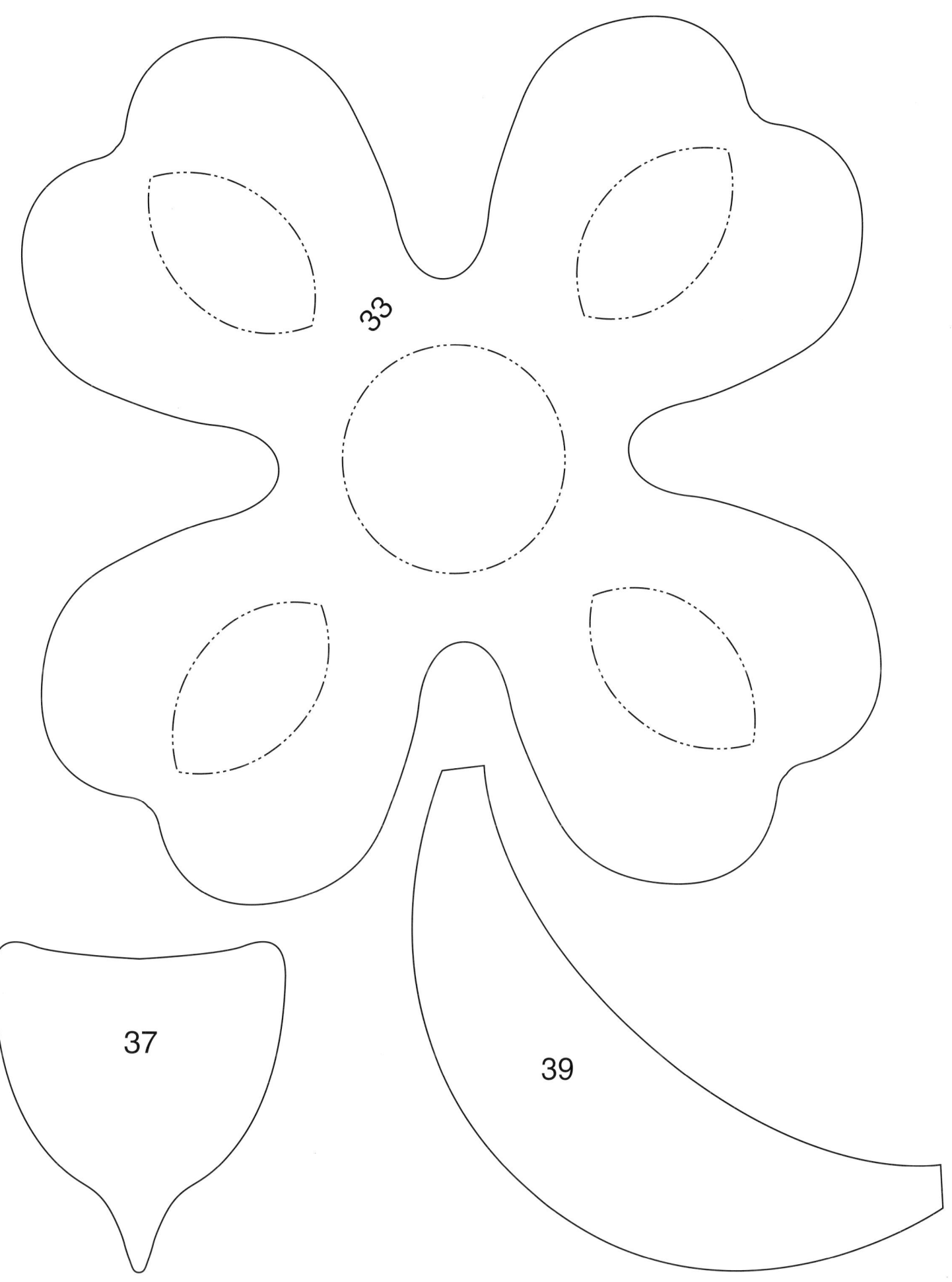

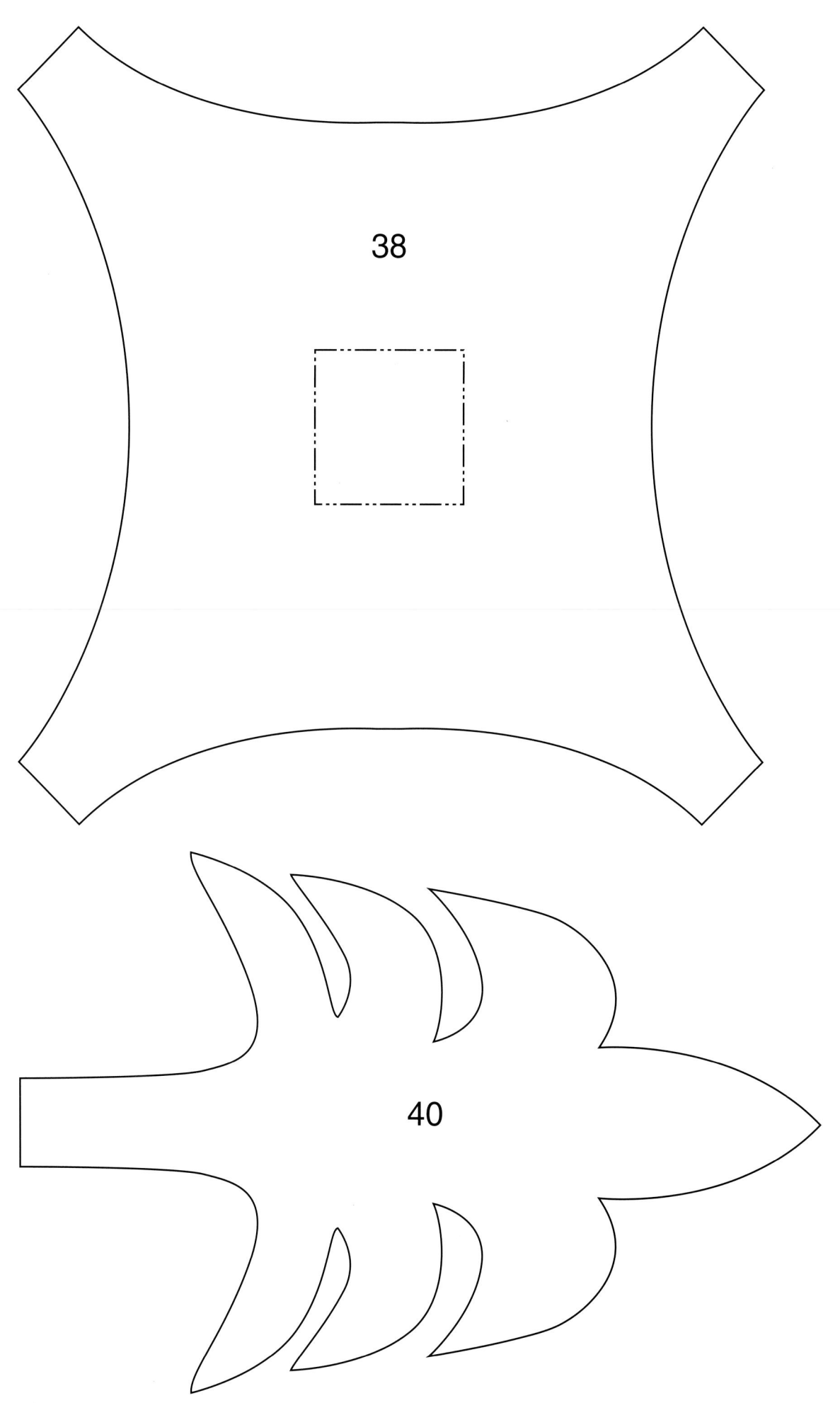

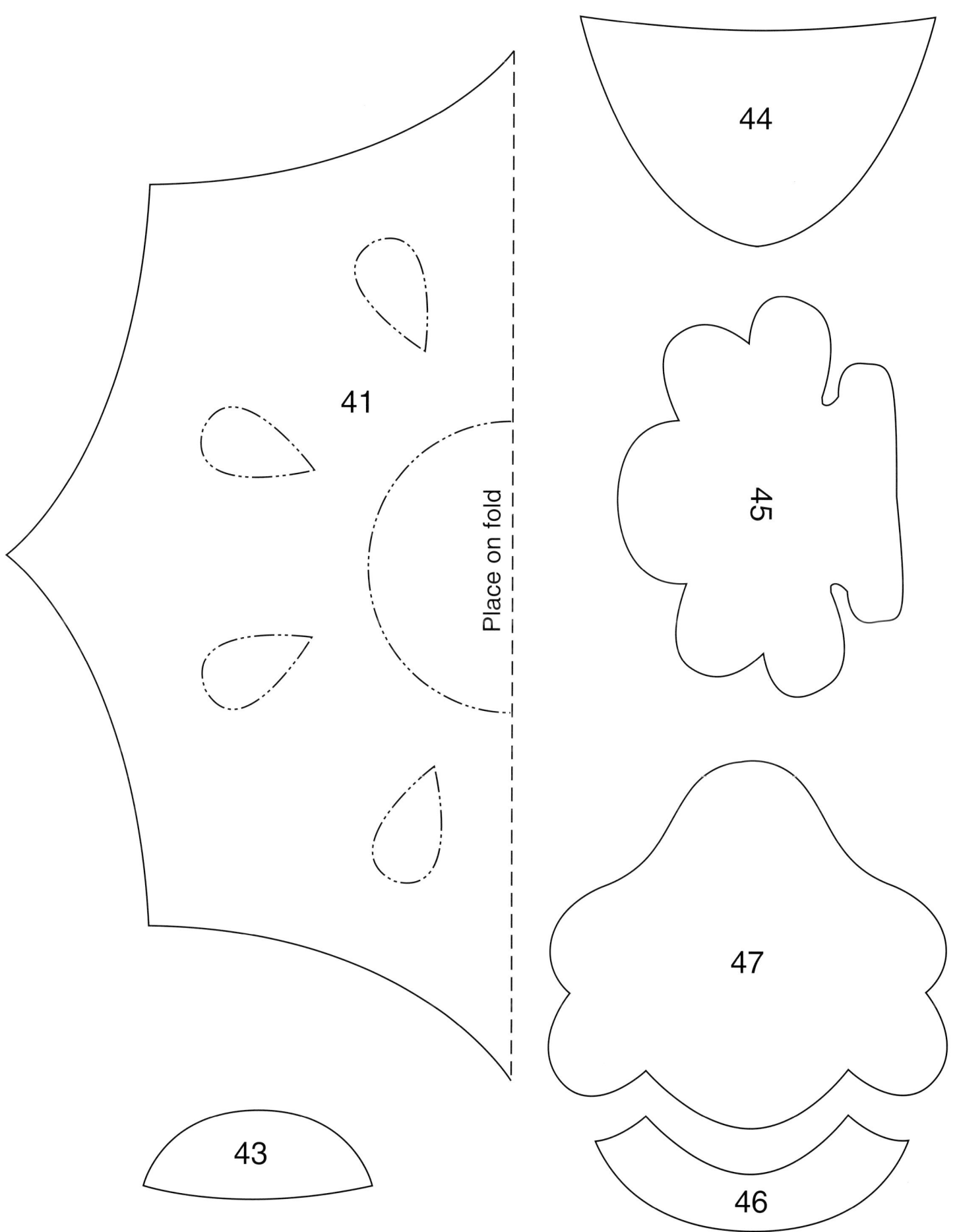

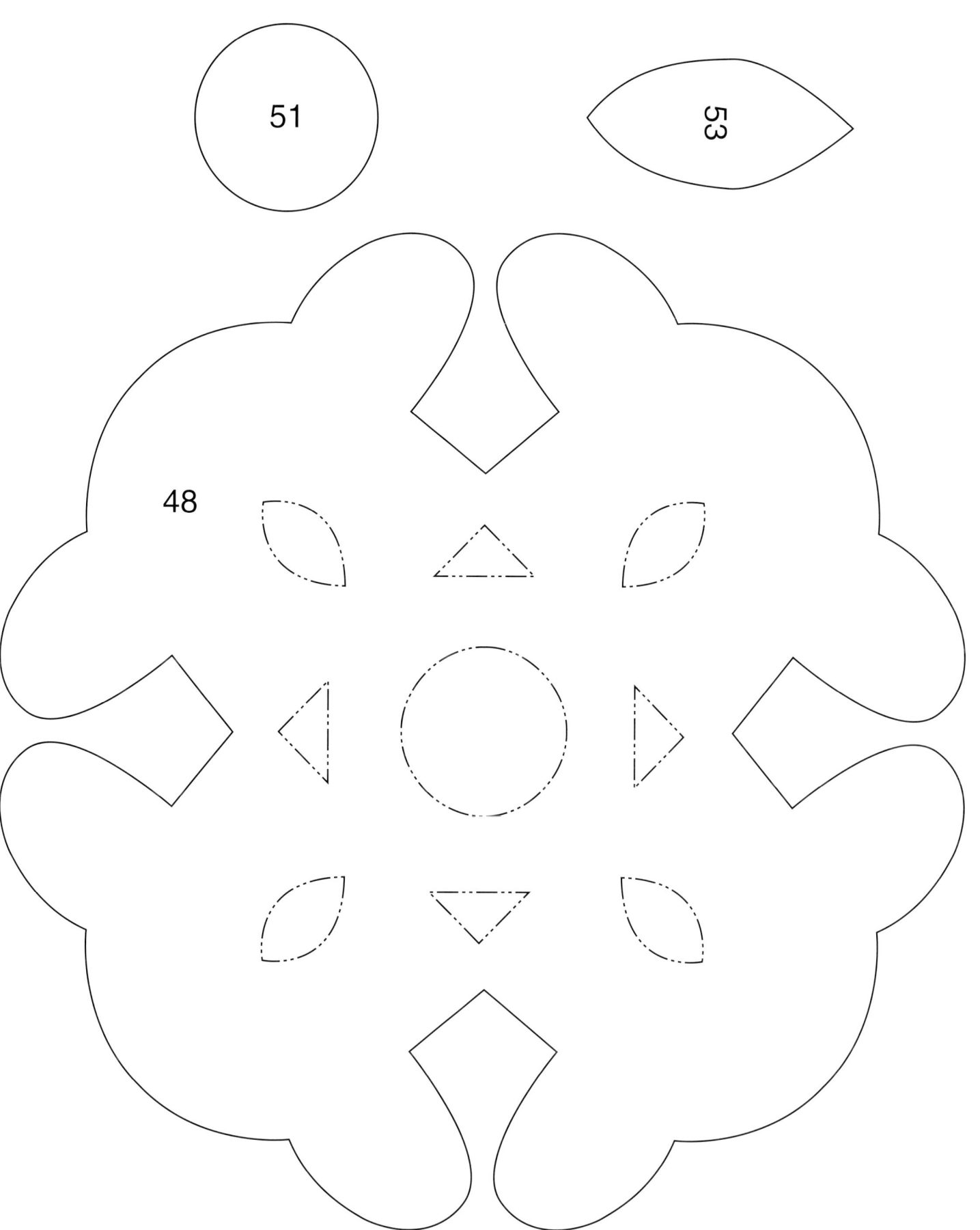

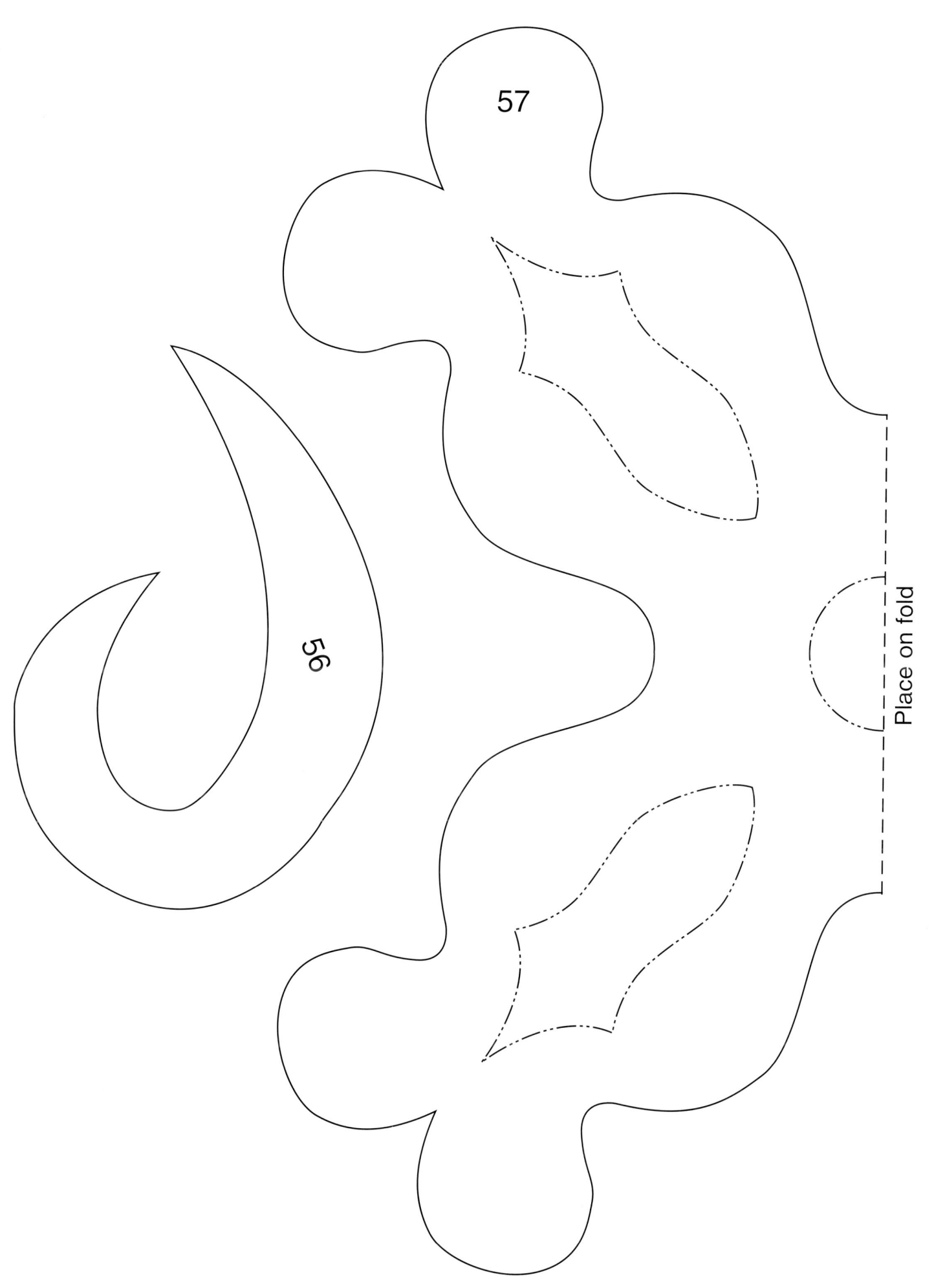

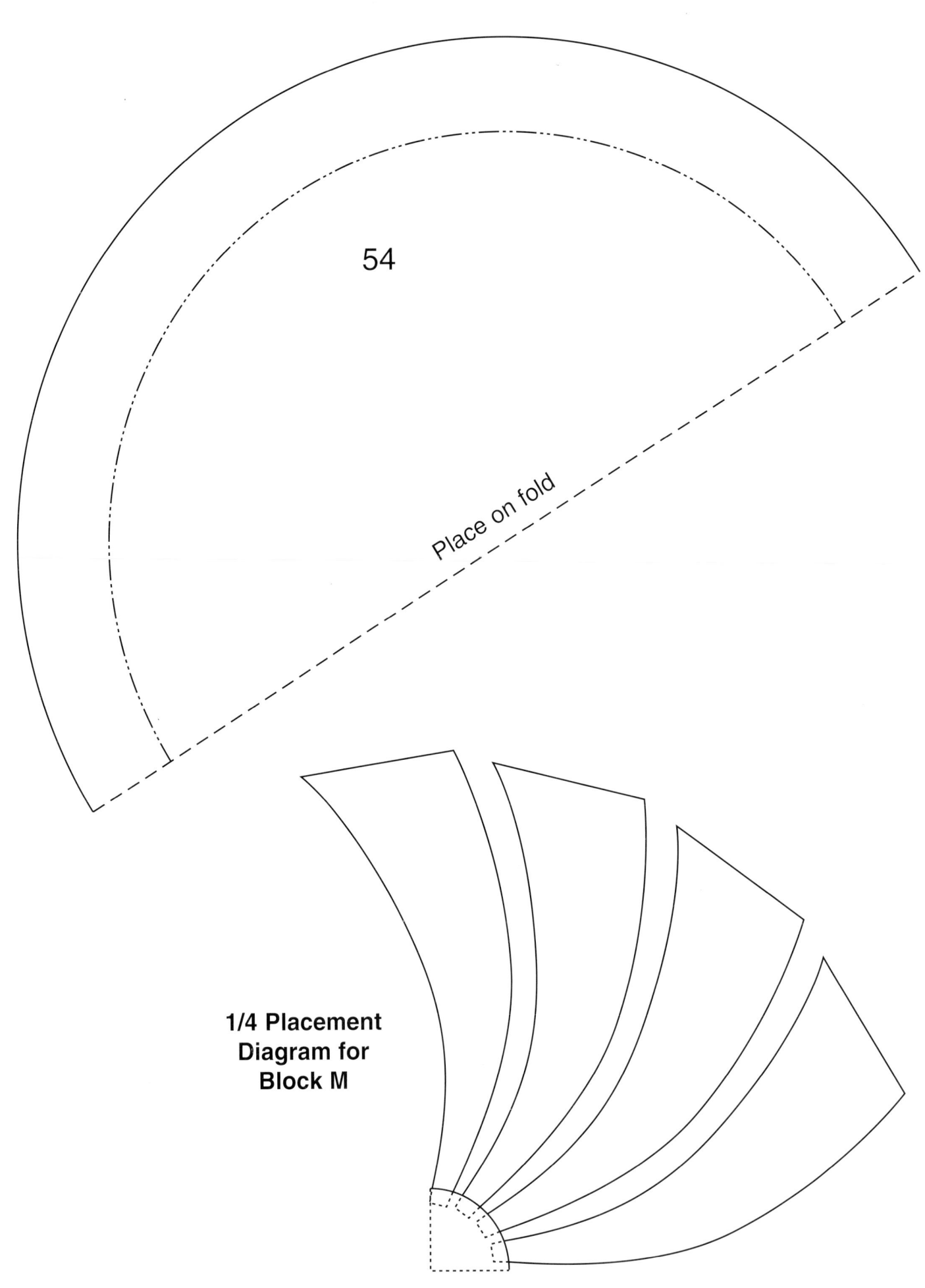